EquineWorks, Inc: Horses Reading People ™
Norco, Mira Loma & Redlands, CA

Life Skills • Problem Solving •
Recovery•Teamwork

Teens•Couples•Families•Groups
www.equineworks.com

Table of Contents

~ Soul Recovery ~

equine assisted activities for healing from abuse by others, loss of others & loss of self

WARNING!

Horses are unpredictable by nature. It is important to understand that the horse's survival instincts are what have allowed the horse to survive from prehistoric times to the present day. It is advised by the authors and EquineWorks, Inc that any participant understand the warnings concerning protective attire and the nature and physical character of the horse before engaging in an equine activity.

Equine activities may result in serious injury or death. Neither the authors nor EquineWorks, Inc assumes any liability for loss or damage, direct or consequential, to the readers, participants, or others resulting from the use of the materials contained herein, whether such loss or damage results from errors, omissions, ambiguities or inaccuracies, negligence or deliberate, in the materials contained herein or otherwise.

About Us

EquineWorks , Inc was formed in 2009 to provide innovative psychotherapy services incorporating the use of horses. The primary base of operation had been on a private ranch located in Norco, California, then, in October, 2011, we entered into an agreement with Queen of Hearts Ranch, located in nearby Mira Loma. This collaboration lead to the availability of more horses, expanded the menu of our services, and the number of clients served. In August, 2011 EquineWorks incorporated as a non profit and in 2012, we will be pursuing various grants & funding options in preparation for federal approval of our tax-exempt status.

Our vision is to provide a mental health treatment option that offers a vehicle for developing life skills and empowerment to heal from life's challenges, through meaningful equine assisted activities.

EquineWorks, Inc currently offers:

- Equine assisted psychotherapy (EAP), a treatment plan based service for all mental health related issues
- Equine assisted learning (EAL); a goal based service for groups wanting to develop team building and leadership skills
- An Introduction to Horses course, for youth and others looking to gain effective communication skills and improve social functioning
- "The Empowered Woman": a six week, two-hour workshop for groups of women focused on learning to trust internal wisdom, developing strategies to face fears, setting personal boundaries and improving communication skills.

Our goal is to serve a wider client base and to go to clients that can not get to us due to economic, geographical or transportation limitations. Currently, we are in Riverside County in the cities of Norco and Mira Loma (Jurupa Valley). We are also in Redlands, within San Bernardino County. We are a 45 minute drive from many locations in both Orange and Los Angeles counties.

Clinical Team

Joy Nussen, LMFT

Joy is the founder and executive director of EquineWorks and has been a California licensed Marriage & Family Therapist since 1991. Joy earned her undergraduate degree in Psychology from the University of California, at Los Angeles and her graduate degree in Educational Psychology from California State University, at Northridge. Since completing EAGALA Part II training in 2008, Joy has gained experience in the equine world by working as a ranch therapist for Childhelp - Merv Griffin Village, in Beaumont, CA and studying with natural horseman, Dale McCarrell, a student of internationally acclaimed horsemen Bill & Tom Dorrance.

Over the years, Joy worked in residential treatment settings with youth in California and Florida, in private practice, in the hospital setting and has had extensive experience in the behavioral health insurance industry on a national level.

Joy is honored to have had her *"Magic Room"* activity, contained within this publication, recently released in the book: *"Harnessing the Power of Equine Assisted Counseling: Adding Animal Assisted Therapy to Your Practice,* released in December, 2011.

'Makena' (Africans for "joyful one") is Joy's domesticated mustang mare. They are currently on a journey to become a confident team so they can navigate the world outside of the ranch arena.

Leslie Becker, LMFT

Leslie joined EquineWorks with 20 years of experience as a California licensed Marriage & Family Therapist and more than 42 years of experience as an equestrian and horse owner. Leslie introduced Joy to EAGALA and they attended the Level 1 training together in 2006.

Leslie earned her undergraduate degree in Psychology and a graduate degree in Educational Psychology from California State University at Northridge. Leslie's 1989 Master's thesis was a project proposal entitled: "Horses as Therapy; Treating Sexually Abused Adolescents."

Now, more than 20 years later, she is proud to contribute some of her activities involving horses to facilitate healing. Her work at EquineWorks is allowing the dream of a graduate student to find expression.

Leslie's passion for horses began at the age of 4-5 when she took horseback riding lessons at a local riding stable in Palm Springs, California. She owned her first horse, "Lady" by the age of 8, and it was then that she discovered the magic of horses as healers. Lady was Leslie's first therapist. She talked to Lady about troubles at home, she was there if Leslie was screaming, laughing or crying. As Leslie relays, "I cried with her soft fur against my cheek and most importantly, when I made mistakes she was always there, unconditionally." During childhood, Leslie and her family traveled the U.S, showing horses on the International Arabian Horse Association Circuit. Leslie is now the proud owner of her first American Quarter Horse.

Leslie's professional focus is on pre and post-natal psychology, which emphasizes support of parents and children from birth to adulthood. Leslie is an active member of the Inland Empire Peri-natal Mental Health Collaborative and she is the co-founder of At Home Family Coaching, addressing the issues of post-partum depression in families. Leslie is also an internationally known therapist and trainer from her work at Dr. Janov's Primal Center in Venice California, where she was for seven years. She worked in association with John Bradshaw at Pasadena Community Hospital dealing with Co-Dependency and Addiction and she has worked with at-risk children in residential and outpatient settings through the local school district as well as in Los Angeles County.

Leslie co-founded Mountain Special Needs 501c3, a small non profit agency in the San Bernardino mountain region providing services to children and their families experiencing a variety of disabilities. Mountain Special Needs was named top new organization of the year 2008-2009 by the local Chamber of Commerce and is a First 5 of San Bernardino community partner.

Personal Notes

What strikes me the most about facilitating an equine assisted psychotherapy (EAP) session is that for the first time in twenty-one years as a mental health professional, I love what I do.

I marvel at literally seeing the development of positive change and healing, and having the honor of being part of that with another. I love being outdoors in the open air and physically moving, versus being glued to a chair at my desk where I've sat for almost ten years doing my behavioral health insurance work. I relish the natural, wild scent of the horses and feeling grounded in mother earth, especially in the company of a mare. I enjoy using my brain to create the activities and it's a bonus that in using my brain in this way, I may help myself to stave off Alzheimer's, which ultimately took my father's life.

I am thrilled that I am able to bring all of me into this innovative practice of mental health treatment and better yet, I cherish the feeling of being free to do so because the standard limitations, pressures and expectations of office-based work, well.. they…vanish.
I am musical, quick-witted and live my life with much humor. I have begun to bring these

elements into my EAP work and I am so very grateful for the opportunity to do so. Bringing all of me to help others become all of whom they are; from where I sit, it just doesn't get any better than that. In turning 50 this year, I have been more in touch with my mortality. I recently found myself drawn to existential psychotherapist, Irvin Yalom's book: Staring at the Sun: Overcoming the Dread of Death. In Dr. Yalom's view, four ultimate concerns are particularly germane to the practice of therapy: death, isolation, meaning in life, and freedom. In my professional and personal maturation, these concerns resonate with me now more than ever.

I am finally digesting the concept of 'internal wisdom' and that my clients have the answers to the questions they bring to therapy. This has become crystal clear because of the images that unfold before my eyes in the horse arena setting - physical, concrete, symbolic and metaphorical representations of the client's inner world that, with my assistance, if I am listening with all senses, transform into a meaningful healing experience.

The equine assisted activities I custom design for my clients set the stage for therapy like no other I have experienced in my career (or in my own therapy) because it is primarily non verbal, non-intrusive, reverent, client-empowering, creative, fun, and gets to the heart of the matter quickly.

I shake my head and pop my eyelids open in disbelief when I hear a teenage client tell me she is "comfortable" and having "fun" in therapy and my heart warms when I witness a family laughing together. What a sharp contrast to the storming-out-of-the-room sessions I experienced when working in an office ! This work makes me a better person because it forces me to be humble and to choose my words carefully before speaking; it requires a great deal of patience, trust in humans, our horses and the unfolding therapeutic process.

Although EquineWorks is in its infancy, we have been fortunate in experiencing life changing client sessions and we have received positive feedback about this amazing work. It is the client that shows us how the "silly" activity we instructed them to do is, in actuality, a profound experience.

We hope the following activities are of help to you. They have been created by two of us at EquineWorks in addressing varying types of abuse and loss; all calling for the recovery if not discovery, of the soul.

~ Joy Nussen
March, 2012

~ The Magic Room ~
an equine assisted activity for the child within a group experience

by: Joy Nussen

"Isolation only exists in isolation. Once shared, it evaporates."

-Irvin Yalom

Introduction

The *magic room* is an activity I created for children and adolescents while working in a residential treatment program. This technique centers on creating and experiencing an emotionally safe space, practicing leadership, an opportunity for expression of feelings through verbal and nonverbal communication, teamwork and sharing, and time to create and imagine.

The youth at this facility came from abusive histories, so issues surrounding safety and trust were my focus. Within the arena, I offered building props (e.g., PVC piping, cones, barrels, logs) and opened a physical space for the child to design a special place where these issues could be addressed.

The horse added the element of a nonjudgmental friend who could navigate this new world with them. A bonus could include self-empowerment for the child, particularly when leading the powerful equine into the created space.

Rationale

As referenced earlier by Dr. Yalom, isolation and freedom are two of the four ultimate concerns particularly germane to the practice of therapy. The magic room activity provides the companionship of the non verbal, non judgmental horse and the freedom for the child to create without interruption or commentary.

Horses are motivated toward basic needs. Because of this very specific motivation, horses keep themselves very focused, healthy, safe and happy. In contrast, children who have not had their basic needs met are easily distracted, do not feel safe, are depressed, angry, or otherwise emotionally disturbed, and are often physically unhealthy. Partnering with a live being who is a positive role model is an ideal solution.

The large size of a horse offers a perfect opportunity for a client to overcome fear and develop confidence. Plus, just like us, horses experience a large variety of emotions and are intuitive and social animals with distinct personalities, attitudes, and moods. They have defined roles within their herds comparable to human dynamics. Because of these similarities, horses can demonstrate and teach self-awareness, honest communication, trust, healthy boundaries, leadership, patience, assertiveness, play, affection, nurturance, and more.

An essential tenet of this work states, "If you have a better understanding of your body language, you have a better understanding of yourself." Horses have the ability to mirror exactly what human body language is telling them, and therefore provide us with metaphors and lessons about ourselves in order to help facilitate change. I observed shifts in physical body posture of the children as they gained confidence in leading this large, majestic creature around the arena. I also witnessed changes in facial expression as fear melted away and the joy of the partnership between the child and the horse developed.

The philosophy of the Equine Assisted Growth and Learning Association (EAGALA) includes believing that clients have the best solutions for themselves and then stepping out of the way so they can discover those solutions (Kersten & Thomas, 2005). In the created space of the magic room, the children felt safe to tell their silent, nonjudgmental friend about their life struggles or for a few precious moments, just to allow themselves the chance to relax in the company of a natural leader.

Description

The group builds a magic room together from a variety of materials available to them in the arena. The definition of *magic room* is decided on by the group (e.g., if the counselor is asked what a magic room is, children are told that it is up to them).

Children choose a horse (may or may not be haltered already) and then take turns entering the 'room' by themselves with their horse. They are told they can stay as long as they want in the room and that if they choose to they can talk privately to their horse.

The remaining children are walking around the arena with their horse, in a different area, in groups of two, taking turns being the leader walking the horse. When participants in the room state that they are ready to exit the room, they change places with one of the clients walking a horse around the arena.

A period of time is offered at the conclusion of the session for those who want to share any of their experiences during the activity. The number of horses used for the magic room depends on group size. This activity may need to be carried over to multiple sessions to enable each participant to be in the magic room. Children may decide to change horses at times, and that can also be an interesting topic to discuss as many children have a difficult time sharing "their" horse.

Materials

- Minimum of 3 horses
- Halters, lead lines
- Building materials for magic room: logs, cones, barrels, pvc piping, swimming pool noodles, etc

Meaningful questions for processing

- How did you decide to build the magic room?
- Was there a leader?
- How did you decide to choose the horse you did?
- What makes the room magic?
- How would it have been different if you didn't have the horse in the room with you?
- Did you choose to speak to your horse? Would you like to share anything about your conversation?
- How would it have been different if you had a person instead of a horse in the room with you?
- Is there anyone you know that you would like to have in the special room with you?
- How did you decide when you were ready to leave the room?
- When is there a time you would like a safe, special space of your own?
- Is there a safe place you can go? How can you make that happen?
- How did you feel being the leader when walking the horse? How about when you weren't the leader?
- What did or didn't you like about this activity?

Application

This activity has a variety of applications and can be used over a period of time depending on group size, children's needs, unexpected individual and group dynamics, and session time allotment. This technique was created for children and adolescents with abusive histories in a residential treatment program but is also applicable to families. The activity can also be conducted in silence. Questions about how the activity was different when talking and not talking can lead to great insight about communication, self-expression, and personal needs. Family work can also be done where members work together or individually.

References

Kersten, G., & Thomas, L. (2005). *Equine Assisted Psychotherapy and Learning Untraining Manual.* Santaquin, UT: Equine Assisted Psychotherapy and Learning Association (EAGALA).

Nussen, J. (2012). The Magic Room. In K. Sudekum Trotter (Ed.), *Harnessing the power of equine assisted counseling: adding animal assisted therapy to your practice.* New York: Routledge/Taylor & Francis Group

Trask, L. (2010). *Helping with horses: Equine assisted psychotherapy (EAP).* Southern Seasons. Retrieved from: www.freshsteps.net/index.html

Yalom, I. (2008). *Staring at the Sun: Overcoming the Dread of Death.* Great Britain: Piatkus Book

~ Snapshot ~
an equine assisted activity for the adult

by: Joy Nussen

Introduction

This activity is an adaptation from *My World* (Cramer, Knapp, Jacoby, and Anthony, 2007, pp. 32-34) and *My Space* (Coleman, 2012, pp. 30-34) and was created out of a client's choice to symbolically construct her life's journey when asked to "build a sacred place." The snapshot metaphor comes from the picture-book image the client portrayed of her life story and my relation to another non-verbal psychotherapeutic modality, sandplay.

Rationale

As referenced earlier by Dr. Yalom, death, meaning in life, isolation and freedom are the ultimate concerns faced in therapy. All are captured in this activity.

Sandplay is a non verbal psychotherapeutic modality developed by the late Swiss psychotherapist Dora Kalff, who gave the child and adult client alike a physically free space (a sand tray) to be unconditionally accepted, to be observed without judgment and to be guided only by observation. The sandplay therapist is receptive but makes minimal comment. It is believed that healing takes place because of the deliberate discouragement of directed thinking. The sand tray becomes a metaphoric sacred ground and because there is no interpretation during sandplay, there is an acceptance of "what is," since there are no rules, nor "right" way to play. The silent capacity to enter into the creation of the client's world with him/her, can, in itself, help repair the feeling of isolation with which so many people are afflicted (Weinrib, 2004, p.33).

In recognizing that symbolic language is the foundation for equine assisted therapies, I enrolled in the University of California at San Diego Professional Program in Sandplay Therapy Studies to learn more.

The Navajo people use ritual sand pictures in ceremonies of healing, primitive tribes drew protective magic circles on the earth, and Swiss psychiatrist Carl Jung, himself, happened upon a healing form of play in 1963 when he played day after day with the earth and stones on the edge of a lake, giving concrete form to his own fantasies.

As my sandplay instructor notes, both sandplay and EAP .."allow a direct expression through the body, and are able to bypass the content of the mind to allow what is unconscious and instinctual to emerge " (Morena, 2012). I find dignity in this work because both the sandplay therapist and the EAP clinician recognize that the client knows how to heal and we know when to get out of the way. As Morena states, "all that is needed really, is a safe and protected space, and a sense of connection and acceptance."

The non-verbal autonomous-supporting process of sandplay is akin to equine assisted psychotherapy and I have come to realize that the horse arena is truly like a very large sandtray with self-discoveries resulting from the unconscious. In this particular case, my client was astonished by what she created in the arena and without thought.

As Weinrib states, "sometimes nourishment from the unconscious arrives miraculously." (p.177)

The collection of miniature figures and small objects available for use in making a sand picture includes a wide variety of symbolic objects necessary to create a world. Morena calls the use of miniatures in the sand 'symbolic language' and states, "as we become aware of symbolic language, we realize how much we understand intuitively, and then begin to see how it opens powerful doorways into areas of the psyche that cannot be accessed any other way" (2012). I am looking forward to broadening the tools and objects available in the arena and experiencing the unfolding dynamics of including the co-facilitating horses!

The sandplay therapist sits in quiet observation of the picture's development and makes a sketch of it to identify its objects for later study. Photographic slides are taken of the picture after the client leaves and are not shown until a mutually agreed upon time and when the client is emotionally strong enough to process the symbolic interpretations of the pictures. In providing a bridge to the world, the sand tray may serve as a transitional object, as defined by analyst D.W. Winnicott. Clients have reported that they carry the sandtray in their head and play things out in it (Weinrib, pp. 54-55). By incorporating the use of a photograph or snapshot, for my client, I hope he/she can take the image and apply what has been learned about oneself outside of the arena.

Description

My client came to me from a traumatic history involving childhood abandonment, a longstanding abusive marriage, the death of her son, a near death accident of her other son, a severe anxiety disorder impacting her ability to drive for decades and current financial distress. For as long as she could remember, she was drawn to horses.

When she read my press release for "The Magic Room," she decided to schedule an appointment with EquineWorks. The following activity is from our second meeting.

Materials

A variety of materials were made available in the arena and I turned out a mare in the arena since the feeling of the day was about female wisdom and the need for female companion-ship. I let the horse figure it out from there, like they always do. I asked my client to build a sacred place, a place she can go to feel safe; but this translated into "build a snapshot of your life."

Case Example

My client built a representation of her sons by using two blue barrels, a daughter she wished she would have had, by a pink swimming pool noodle, and caution ended her path that lead to the barrels, as represented by two orange cones and two logs, respectively. We talked about her life story and when I asked if she would adjust anything to create the next part of her life or where she wanted to go next, she immediately moved the logs that lined her path to a parallel position along side the barrels and stated she could remain a mother to her sons but also have her own life. I then asked if she would like to take the mare down her new path with her and she did so. After several passes through the path, she continued to walk with the horse around the arena until she felt she was ready to conclude. An interesting observation was that the path was narrow so only the horse was able to walk through it, leaving my client on the other side of the path guiding the horse. It would have been interesting to ask what it would have meant to her, if anything, to change the width of the path.

In this simple but powerful activity that truly unfolded on its own, all the issues this client brought to therapy were touched upon in a brief period of time: the death of her son and how to find meaning in continuing on in her life as a mother to her other son, reaching out from her isolation and finding freedom to be herself.

When my client arrived at her third session, she told me her panic symptoms related to driving had diminished significantly. When I asked what she thought this was due to, she said she was feeling empowered for the first time in a long time, from the interaction with the horses and by allowing herself to do something enjoyable, just for her.

Meaningful questions for processing

- How did you choose this image of your life versus another?
- How does it feel to share this snapshot of your life?
- Are there regrets you built?
- How can you live now without building new regrets?
- What do you think has to change in your life?
- What did it feel like to have the horse with you?
- If you were to name the horse, who/what would it be?
- Is there someone with whom you would like to share this image/these images?

Application

This activity started as one idea and transformed into something else; we need to be flexible with this work! Asking the client to portray or construct a snapshot of their life can be a powerful exercise.

Concepts inherent in the sandplay process include the taking of photographs so that the client can have a record of their insightful moment and a "bridge to the world" for on-going development outside the arena. When to take the snapshots and when to discuss them needs to be reviewed and discussed with the client. As in the sandplay process, it is important to respect the integrity of the client's work by not dismantling it in his/her presence.

There are many options on how to incorporate the horse or horses in this activity. I chose to offer one 'female friend' to accompany my client on her journey.

My particular client's issues include the traumatic grief of losing her son. Entering into a discussion about death involves empathy but it also requires personal work by the therapist. It is a professional responsibility to know your own grief and loss issues and, where you are psychically in regards to death and dying, before agreeing to work with clients facing these issues.

Broadening the tools and objects available in the arena to create a large sandtray-type environment is an interesting prospect and challenge. I will have fun exploring it and I hope you do too...

References

Cramer, K., Knapp, S., Jacoby, R., & Anthony, L. (2007). Girls rule: An 8-week EAP group for adolescent girls ages 11-15. Marshall, N.C.: Horse Sense of the Carolinas, Inc.

Coleman, V. (2012). Reclaiming boundaries through equine assisted counseling. In K. Sudekum Trotter (Ed.), *Harnessing the power of equine assisted counseling: adding animal assisted therapy to your practice.* New York: Routledge/Taylor & Francis Group

Morena, G. (2012). In an email conversation.

Weinrib, E. (2004).*The Sandplay Therapy Process: Images of the Self.* Cloverdale, CA: Temenos Press

Yalom, I. (2008). *Staring at the Sun: Overcoming the Dread of Death.* Great Britain: Piatkus Books

~ Breaking the Silence ~
an equine assisted activity for the sexually
abused adolescent: indifferent type

by: Leslie Becker

Introduction

When I wrote my thesis in 1989, the sexual abuse
of children had been virtually ignored in
psychological literature. Professionals, as well as
the public, were hesitant to acknowledge the
scope and severity of the problem. Until the early
1970's, child sexual abuse was thought to be rare,
and centered among the poor. Experts now agree
that child sexual abuse has always occurred and
still exists in all socio-economic groups. Increased
public awareness has led to greater reporting;
from 1970 to 1990, child sexual abuse reports
increased more than other categories of neglect or
abuse (National Research Counsel, 1993). Despite
this gain, child sexual abuse still remains vastly
under-reported.

Rationale

Sexual abuse occurs in rural, urban and suburban areas and among all ethnic, racial and socioeconomic groups (NRCCSA, 1994). Most children are abused by someone they know and trust, although boys are more likely than girls to be abused outside of the family (AMA, March, 1992). Children are most vulnerable between ages eight-12 (Finkelhor et al, 1986). The average age for first abuse is 9.9 years for boys and 9.6 years for girls (NRCCSA, 1994). Victimization occurs before age eight in over 20 percent of the cases. Another study found 24 percent of female child sexual abuse survivors were first abused at age five or younger (Boyer and Fine, Jan. 1992). Gay, lesbian and bisexual youth may be at greater risk because they tend to be socially isolated and are easier targets (Savin-Williams vol. 62, no. 2 1994).

Sexual abuse survivors are at higher risk for mental health and social functioning problems resulting from feelings of powerlessness, guilt, shame, stigmatization and low self-esteem (Finkelhor et al, 1986). Powerlessness damages coping skills and reduces ability to protect oneself from further abuse.

Psychological and behavioral effects of child sexual abuse may include low self-esteem, depression, anxiety, fear, hostility, chronic

33

tension, eating disorders, sexual dysfunction, self-destructive or suicidal behavior, post traumatic stress disorder, dissociation, multiple personality disorder, repeat victimization, running away, criminal behavior, academic problems, substance abuse and prostitution.

General styles of behaving described as *"typologies"* are chosen by the adolescent as a means to cope with the consequence of being a victim of sexual abuse. These typologies are behaviors incorporated in the adolescent's personality as a defense. The typologies described are: Hostile/Aggressive, Withdrawn/Indifferent, and Pseudo Adaptive. Treatment and activities are designed to address two of these typologies to facilitate change on the cognitive, developmental and behavioral level.

Horse Facilitated Psychotherapy™ (HFP), as described in my master's thesis from 1989, was inspired by my personal experience and intuition that horses are amazing loving animals that have an unlimited ability to teach life lessons and love unconditionally.

The horse as a therapeutic agent first appeared in writing in early mythology, beginning with Chiron, the centaur (half man, half horse), known as the first physician and teacher of Aesculapius. Aesculapius is said to have prescribed riding for people with wounds and diseases that would not heal. HFP is an action therapy designed around the care, maintenance, and riding of horses. Specific developmental crises parallel the interactions between horses and humans and I indicate how this special interaction can help adolescents increase the ability to delay gratification, exercise patience, carry out responsibilities, and to recognize the needs of others.

In a sense, HFP may be considered as one form of reality therapy. Horses may help to fulfill two basic psychological needs of clients as stated by Glasser (1965): "the need to love and to be loved and the need to feel that we are worthwhile to ourselves and to others".

The success of HFP is based on the proposition that many clients may accept the love of an animal before they can accept love from and give love to another human.

In the beginning, especially with children, the horse and child do not differentiate. The child like the infant does not experience the horse as separate from self. The child and horse begin to communicate silently through nonverbal body language. The language between human and horse is like the language between mother and infant - nonverbal, a silent language expressed through the body. The horse/human interaction initially is very similar to the infant that must rely on a caretaker. The horse is completely dependent upon the human for food, shelter, and contact sensations. As the relationship develops, the horse/human interaction is marked by the child's observation that the horse is separate.

The transition from sameness to separateness seems to take place because the child's intellectual process includes the realization that the horse is separate.

Separation and individuation with the horse takes place for the adolescent much like the infant, who in the second half of the first year, begins to recognize the difference between self and others or self and mother (Winnicott, 1953, 1971).

When in captivity, horses are dependent upon man to care for their daily needs of food and water. Allowing an adolescent to care for and interact with a horse will give them a chance to move away from ego centricity and feel needed by another living creature. The horse/human interaction gives the adolescent a chance to look at their own needs and whether or not they were met in a healthy manner. The adolescent can begin to see themselves by the way the horse responds to their treatment. For example, if the adolescent is kind to the horse and the horse is kind or affectionate back, the adolescent will identify with kind feelings. If the adolescent is aggressive and punishing, and the horse acts fearful and shies away, the child must look at themselves to see what they did to elicit such behavior.

It is through this immediate but non-threatening feedback that the horse gives the child a mirror to see themselves and an opportunity opens for the therapist to process maladaptive behavior adopted as a result of being sexually abused.

Resistance and adolescence go hand in hand and silence, or the refusal to talk to a therapist, is common when an adolescent is brought to therapy. It has been my experience that the resistant adolescent will *"break the silence"* with the horse and entrust long held secrets to the horse who will act as the conduit to the therapist. Thus begins the repair of the first developmental phase that was broken for a sexually abused person: Trust vs. Mistrust.

There are three essential components to a program using (HFP): the horse, the client, and the therapist or treatment team (as in the EAGALA model). I believe we must not ignore that this technique takes place outdoors; this allows for the healing properties of nature to also be included.

The Horse

The selection of horses is of great importance and the following must be considered: the age, the temperament and character, size and conformation. The age of the horse is important because often times a client will have had no horse experience. Young horses are *NOT* the best match for a therapy program. Seasoned horses that are older and that have been exposed to many situations are often best suited for a therapy program. This will help ensure the safety of all persons especially the fearful, young abused adolescent. Older, well trained or broke horses between the ages of 7-15 would be ideal for this type of therapy. A horse that has any history of biting or kicking someone must not be used. Older horses can also be valuable to a program because of their maturity, experience and calmness. Horses of this age definitely have minds of their own and are easier to evaluate for their appropriateness for this type of work. The horse, like the adolescent, has adopted a style of behaving.

Knowing your horses is important when making matches between horse and client. The horse chosen as a therapy aid must appeal to the client/adolescent and be appropriate to the psychodynamics of each resident. Boris Levinson believes that children that have been emotionally "burned", resent authority and being pushed, and hence prefer a pet which is unobtrusive, independent, not demonstrative in its affection, and not apt to initiate or seek a friendship (Levinson, 1979, p. 76).

Many horses fit these characteristics perfectly, making them an excellent match for any abused person. Size and conformation must be considered when making a match with each client. Some clients will be much better suited to a larger or smaller horse. For example, the hostile/aggressive behavior type will be less able to intimidate a larger horse. The withdrawn/indifferent behavior type may be better matched to a smaller horse initially. Conformation and soundness may be more important during different activities.

The Client

Although some adolescents may have had pets in their lives or in rare instances, experience with horses, it is not a requirement for this approach. A complete history is important to know if the client has any history of animal abuse. Accepting a client with a history of animal abuse must be evaluated on case by case bases.

The Therapist/Horse Specialist

Selection of the mental health professional and equine specialist will demand they are highly qualified in each of their specific professions. I happen to qualify to be either so as a team member I can shift positions.

Grooming: Building a Relationship

The grooming of horses is extremely important to their health and well being. Grooming involves a thorough examination of the horse and will provide an opportunity to look for any minor injuries or areas on the body that need attention. This activity requires an intimate relationship and brings the adolescent into closer contact with the animal.
The topic of grooming brings into focus how we care for ourselves and also how touch can be both nurturing and or abusive. The horse, in the

grooming relationship, will serve to strengthen the adolescent's ability in investing feelings in others and will help the adolescent become aware of cause and effect relationships. One of the *golden rules* of this approach is to "do unto the horses as you would like others to do unto you".

Breaking the Silence

The goal of this activity is interaction. Grooming is a great activity for the Withdrawn/Indifferent client because he/she communicates primarily non-verbally. The activity of grooming allows the child to approach the horse through their senses. The horse can serve as a bridging object so the adolescent can form a relationship first with the horse, then with the instructor/therapist, and as trust develops, with peers and others.

Materials

1 or more horses, halter, brushes (soft bristle, stiff bristle and a mane/tail brush)

Instruction

Ask the client to choose a horse (if there is more than one) and to attach a halter on "somehow" and lead it to a grooming area. Ask the client to secure the horse in the grooming area then to choose a brush and begin to brush the animal. The therapist may assist getting the halter on the horse and securing it in the grooming area. The brushes are all available for the client to choose. The focus for this activity is on the grooming; not other challenges such as catching the horse or securing it.

The animal can be approached without words and the adolescent can begin to communicate non-verbally with the horse. Levinson strongly advocates pet therapy with children that are non-verbal, autistic, inhibited, and withdrawn (Levinson, 1969a). *"Can I Touch You?"* can be the beginning of the withdrawn/indifferent adolescent's attempt to reach out once again to another living creature and relinquish her protective, silent stance. The horse provides non-threatening contact for the adolescent who has chosen to withdraw from a painful adult world filled with physical and psychological abuse.

The relationship between the horses and adolescent must be established first to bridge a path of communication between the adolescent and the instructor/therapist. It is often observed with this typology that they will begin to talk to the horse as they groom. They will trust their thoughts and feelings first to the horse.

This activity allows for the resistant adolescent to move out of silence and be brought into relationship first with the horse and secondly with the therapist. With this type of adolescent, the therapist will begin his or her involvement as an empathic supporter of the new relationship between horse and client. Creating a supportive and safe environment to establish this new relationship is the therapist's role. The withdrawn or indifferent adolescent needs to regain a sense that the world is a safe place to act and react.

Meaningful questions for processing

- How did you go about haltering and securing the horse? How did those methods work/not work? Did the horse care?
- Did you help the horse today? How so?
- How does a horse communicate without words?

- Does a horse have feelings? How can you tell? How can someone tell if you have feelings?
- In what ways did the horse respond differently when you were brushing him/her?
- Did you ever feel you were brushing too hard or too soft?
- In what ways does a horse need us?
- In what ways do we need one another?

Application

This activity involves catching, haltering, securing the horse and grooming; the latter of which is the actual focus. These elements can be broken up into multiple sessions or the horse can be pre set for grooming when the client arrives for session.

Other options may be to assist the client in various stages leading up to the grooming activity or leaving it up to the client to decide, entirely. Allowing the adolescent to "choose" a horse gives them a sense of control and power.

These activities are directed at treating trauma associated with sexual abuse in adolescent girls but they are appropriate to use with anyone who has experienced trauma and/or where the self/soul has been violated.

References

American Medical Association, March, 1992. *Diagnostic and Treatment Guidelines on Child Sexual Abuse.* Chicago, AMA.

Boyer, D, Fine, D. vol. 24, no. 1, Jan 1992. "Sexual Abuse as a Factor in Adolescent Pregnancy and Child Maltreatment." *Family Planning Perspectives.*

Finkelhor, D. et al, (1986) *A Sourcebook on Child Sexual Abuse,* Newbury Park: Sage Publications.

Glasser, W. (1965). Reality Therapy. New York: Harper & Row.

Levinson, B. M. (1969). Pet Orientated Child Psychotherapy. Springfield, IL.: Charles C. Thomas.

Levinson, B. M. (1980). The Child and His Pet: A World of Nonverbal Communication. In S. A. Corson & E. O'L. Corson (Ed.) Ethnology & Nonverbal Communication in Mental Health. (pp. 63-81). New York: Pergamon Press.

National Research Council . (1993). *Understanding Child Abuse Neglect,* Washington, DC: National Academy Press.

Ritch Savin-Williams. (1994). "Verbal and Physical Abuse as Stressors in the Lives of Lesbian, Gay Male and Bisexual Youths: Associations School Problems, Running Away, Substance Abuse, Prostitution and Suicide," *Journal of Consulting and Clinical Psychology, vol.* 62, no. 2.

The National Resource Center on Child Sexual Abuse. (1994). "Fact Sheet on Child Sexual Abuse," Huntsville: NRCCSA.

Winnicott, D. W. (1953). Transitional Objects and Transitional Phenomena. International Journal of Psychoanalysis, 24, p. 88-97.

Winnicott, D. W. (1971). Therapeutic Consultations in Child Psychiatry. Basic Books.

~ Take A Hold of Me ~
an equine assisted activity for the sexually
abused adolescent: pseudo adaptive type

by: Leslie Becker & Joy Nussen

Rationale

The sexually abused child may feel he or she is
not an acceptable member of society. Children
who have experienced sexual abuse can feel
alienated, marked by their experience, and may
struggle with daily feelings of incompetence and
low self-worth.

According to Wikipedia, the greek prefix,
"pseudo" is used to mark something as
fraudulent or pretending to be something it is not
and "adaptive" is defined as a type of behavior
used to adjust to another type of behavior or
situation. The pseudo adaptive teen appears to
outside observers such as teachers, parents and
friends to "have it all together." This type usually
functions according to established rules and does
not "rock the boat."

This client has learned how to be "good" and to fly below the radar externally, while emotionally crashing internally under the weighted burden of pretending.

The behavioral characteristics of the pseudo adaptive type client may only come to our attention after a crisis. The crisis may be enough to breakdown the facade of a strong, confident, "got it all together" adolescent.

The pseudo adaptive adolescent/client coming into treatment can be expected to exhibit some or all of the following behavioral characteristics:

- expresses feelings indirectly
- resistance is expressed indirectly, i.e., procrastination
- has a desire for affection and acceptance, allows people to only see "good" side
- humiliation or emptiness in response to criticism
- low self-esteem; devalues self-achievements and is overly dismayed by personal shortcomings
- a belief that core of self is bad
- over-idealizes people

You see what you get with a horse; there are no falsehoods or personas. When a new horse joins an established herd, there is indeed a period of adjustment. Once a horse has been accepted by the herd, however, roles become clearly defined and daily living is focused on protection, survival and companionship.

Observing the Herd & Haltering Easy vs Hard to Catch Horses ~

Catching and haltering a horse who wants to cooperate in doing so is a very different experience from when a horse doesn't want to participate in that activity. The pseudo adaptive client may want it to appear as though there is no big challenge in front of them. Being vulnerable and needing help is a sign of weakness for these clients.

The differing personalities and behaviors in the herd environment can mirror the social dynamics of human interaction and can be a non threatening playground for us to explore different parts of ourselves.

Materials

- several turned out horses in a large arena or pasture, at least 1 difficult to catch and 1 easy to catch horse
- halters of various styles and sizes with lead ropes

Instruction

Choose one of these pieces of equipment and choose a horse that represents you. The equipment must be secured on the horse in order for you to be able to lead the horse anywhere you wish in this space.

The pseudo adaptive type will have to be carefully observed for "faking it"; they want and need to look "good" and will rarely ask for help. This characteristic can be extremely dangerous when considering the potential for injury when dealing with horses.

Once the client has achieved affixing the halter to the horse, they are now connected. The horse creates an extension for the client who can experience their social environment in a new way. All sexually abused clients deal with feeling of powerlessness.

This activity can assist them in exploring how to harness their power by experiencing genuine horse power.

Application

This activity can be used with a variety of presenting issues and age groupings. Entering the horse herd environment as a human student offers much education and feeling a new sense of power in catching that "difficult horse" offers us the opportunity to increase our confidence and to cease acting offensively in order to feel safe. Bonding for the pseudo adaptive client is likely a new experience and the feeling of being part of a welcoming group is healing indeed.

Meaningful questions for processing

- What were the decisions you made today in choosing your halter and horse?
- What do you think the herd thought of you?
- When do you think someone should ask for help?
- What are the different roles the horses play in this herd?
- What horses were like you and which horses weren't like you?
- How are these horses' lives different or the same from a group of people hanging out together?

- Which horse is the most liked in this herd?
- Which horse is the most afraid?
- Which horse is the bravest?

~ Life Skills ~
an equine assisted activity for the teen client family

by: Joy Nussen

Introduction

This activity is an adaptation from *My World*
(Cramer, Knapp, Jacoby, and Anthony, 2007, pp.
32-34) and created from the idea to incorporate a
parent into the EAGALA team in order to
promote the parent's sense of value to the family.

Rationale

Carl Rogers, a pioneer in psychotherapy research,
demonstrated that improvement in therapy was
associated with the therapist's characteristics of
genuineness, accurate empathy, and unconditional
regard. The concept of genuineness takes on a more
far reaching meaning for existential issues, per
master psychotherapist, Irvin Yalom. "Work on
empathy is bidirectional: not only must you
experience the patient's world, but you must also
help patients develop their own empathy for others.
(p. 241). I found this point resonated well for this
client given her issues and age.

Just like us, horses experience a large variety of emotions and are social animals with distinct personalities, attitudes, and moods. Comparable to human socialization and life challenges, they have to adapt to change and to navigate their roles in fluctuating herd dynamics. Horses can raise our awareness of how we stand in judgment of others, attempt to control others, and avoid our responsibilities.

Parents are often already equipped to address many of the challenges that bring them and their families into treatment. This activity is designed to remind them.

Case Example

Parents of a 14 year-old girl came to EquineWorks with concerns over their daughter's social anxiety, difficulties adapting to change, academic struggles, depressed mood, lack of peer relationships and impaired communication skills. Office based therapy was not previously productive and because of the girl's love of horses, EquineWorks appeared to be worth a try.

In genuine support of anything they can do to help, dad and two older brothers also joined the sessions.

Mom, viewed as the "glue" of the family, was unavailable to attend one of the sessions so I chose to design an activity highlighting dad's strengths and wisdom that he could impart to his children with hope that it would address the girl's specific treatment needs we had developed during our initial session.

Dad successfully worked for thirty years as a firefighter and earned promotions through the ranks eventually leading to the position of Deputy Fire Chief. He was forced to retire early due to an injury and was struggling himself in search of his value since this dramatic life changing event, four years prior.

I gave dad a few minutes to think of three life skills he learned during his career and under what circumstances he learned them. The skills he chose were *tolerance, trusting others and facing responsibilities*. Each skill was written on a piece of duct tape and I called on each of the three children to take one skill and attach it as a label to one of three buckets containing horse pellets that had been set aside for the activity.

A hoola hoop was provided for each child who was given instructions to stand inside their hoop somewhere inside the arena and to protect their individual buckets, not allowing the horses to eat from them. I asked dad to join the EAGALA team and at intervals that felt appropriate, we turned out one of three horses.

As the session progressed, I asked dad to think of one characteristic that would get in the way of each of the skills developing or being maintained for someone. For tolerance, he chose standing in *judgment of others*, for trusting others he chose *controlling others*, and for facing responsibilities he chose *procrastination*. Each characteristic was written on duct tape pieces and I asked dad to affix them to each of the horses, as he saw fit.

As we watched together, I asked dad what he was observing with his children as well as with the horses. Interestingly, the only "value bucket" that got invaded by any of the horses belonged to the daughter. This was one of many observations discussed during processing.

Also incorporated into processing was dad sharing the stories behind the skills he had learned; the ones I had asked him to think about earlier. I was in hope that this would serve the dual purpose of dad finding meaning in the sharing of his wisdom with his children and for specifically the daughter to gain insight into the issues that brought her to therapy. The horses did their job by mirroring the energy of the activity participants and doing what comes naturally.

An interesting note is that the girl remarked she was frustrated when the horse ate from her bucket but she did not overtly show frustration. Her brothers remarked during processing that in contrast, it is obvious at home when their sister feels frustrated, as indicated by her words and behavior. When we asked the teen why she thought that was so, she indicated that she felt more relaxed at the ranch.

Materials

- 3 buckets of equal size containing horse feed
- 3 hoola hoops
- Easy to tear duct tape & permanent marker
- 3 or more horses

Meaningful questions for processing

- What was it like to protect your bucket?
- How did you feel toward the horses in this activity?
- What decisions did you make during this activity? Did you change your mind? Why?
- Would you do anything differently if you repeated this activity?
- Would you want to do this activity alone, with the same participants or with someone else next time?
- Were you aware of being observed? Do you think that affected anything?
- Did this activity remind you of anything in your life?
- Did any of the horses represent something for you?
- How did you feel when the horse ate/didn't eat from your bucket?
- How was your reaction different or the same to how you may respond with a frustration in your life? If different, why?
- How was it for you to see the horses eating/not eating from the other participants' buckets?

Application

The identified client in this case came to therapy with issues related to social anxiety, academic struggles, depressed mood, lack of peer relationships and impaired communication skills. Father's life learned skills of *tolerance, trusting others and facing responsibilities* are an anecdote for addressing the majority of these issues and standing in *judgment of others*, trying to *control others*, and *procrastination* are indeed struggles for the daughter.

This client will be best served by being offered Leslie's grooming activity as a starting point in learning about patience/tolerance, trust, appropriate boundary setting and caretaking for another/personal responsibility. Because this client has difficulties articulating her feelings, the non verbal interaction with the horse will assist her in easing into using her words.

There are a multitude of life skills to draw from and a variety of ways to apply this activity. This particular client represents the child who is struggling to find herself.

All (the clinical team and the horses) modeling empathy will hopefully translate into the client's ability and desire to do the same outside the arena so that her mood and relationships improve. The skills of other family members need to be highlighted and utilized in this effort.

References

Cramer, K., Knapp, S., Jacoby, R., & Anthony, L. (2007). Girls rule: An 8-week EAP group for adolescent girls ages 11-15. Marshall, N.C.: Horse Sense of the Carolinas, Inc.

Yalom, I. (2008). *Staring at the Sun: Overcoming the Dread of Death*. Great Britain: Piatkus Books

How Come & Why Now?

While technology has blessed our lives in numerous ways, it frequently isolates us, keeps us out of touch with our true selves and further from "nature." We are texting and instant-messaging instead of face-to-face communicating and our loved ones are having an increasingly difficult time knowing how to talk directly with one another. Our equine-assisted activities create opportunities for improving communication skills and re-connecting.

Due to the state of the economy and with so many unemployed, there are increased feelings of hopelessness and more than ever, a need for creative problem solving. Our equine assisted activities create opportunities to gain insight into one's coping strategies and to think outside "the box." Alcohol and drug abuse/ dependency are societal issues that deepen with increased job, relationship and home loss we face during the hardships of a struggling economy. Our equine-assisted activities create opportunities to face our addictions creatively and without judgment.

Impulse control and anger management issues in our personal lives and at the work place are heightened concerns during a weakening economy. Our equine-assisted activities create opportunities to cool our jets, take a breather and learn adaptive coping skills. Job dissatisfaction drains our economy further due to decreased work performance or missed work days. Employers are often out of touch with the poor morale of those that report to them and during this telecommuting age, many employers have never even met their workers. Our equine-assisted activities create opportunities for morale boosting and corporate team building experiences.

Joy Nussen, LMFT, EAGALA Certified   Leslie Becker, LMFT
joynussen@equineworks.com   lesliebecker@equineworks.com

"There is something about the outside of a horse that is good for the inside of a man."   ~ *Winston Churchill*

EquineWorks, Inc: Horses Reading People ™
Norco, Mira Loma & Redlands, CA USA
(949) 422-6355
www.equineworks.com

Made in the USA
Middletown, DE
09 November 2016